MW00906762

REMEMBERING
JEFFREY

REMEMBERING JEFFREY

Stephanie Howe
As told to Carol Olsen

iUniverse, Inc.
New York Lincoln Shanghai

REMEMBERING JEFFREY

Copyright © 2007 by Stephanie B. Howe

All rights reserved. No part of this book may be used or reproduced by any means, graphic, electronic, or mechanical, including photocopying, recording, taping or by any information storage retrieval system without the written permission of the publisher except in the case of brief quotations embodied in critical articles and reviews.

iUniverse books may be ordered through booksellers or by contacting:

iUniverse
2021 Pine Lake Road, Suite 100
Lincoln, NE 68512
www.iuniverse.com
1-800-Authors (1-800-288-4677)

The views expressed in this work are solely those of the author and do not necessarily reflect the views of the publisher, and the publisher hereby disclaims any responsibility for them.

ISBN: 978-0-595-44324-6 (pbk)
ISBN: 978-0-595-88654-8 (ebk)

Printed in the United States of America

Contents

1989

This is the true story of Jeffrey Eidson, a foundling child, given the name Jeffrey Lopez by his finder and assigned the birth date October 6, 1989 by The Republic of the Philippines Regional Trial Court, 7th Judicial Region, Branch 21 of Cebu City, Philippines.

My husband, Rodney, and I were told that Jeffrey was found in a public market near a toilet around 9:30 in the morning. Jeffrey, presumed to be just one day old, was given over to the authorities and would later be declared "an abandoned, neglected, and dependent child" by the regional director of the Department of Social Welfare and Development.

Jeffrey's discovery was reported to the local police station. He was registered as a foundling with the Local Civil Registrar of Toledo City, Cebu on October 6, 1989. On January 11, he was admitted to the Reception and Study Center for Children, a state run orphanage. Where he spent his first three months of life remains a mystery. Our best guess is that he was in the hospital.

Jeffrey spent his first years at the state run childcare facility of the Department of Social Welfare and Development. This facility's stated mission was to "provide temporary care and shelter to the abandoned, neglected, orphaned and dependent children of Region VII."

Jeffrey's assigned room had ten cribs. Each crib held two babies. The room was approximately 15' by 20'. There was usually just one staff member on duty to care for all of the infants. Jeffrey willed his own survival during those early years. He learned to exert his temper to get attention. He could scream and cry and carry on for hours until someone picked him up. His strong will would remain with him always.

On December 19, 1992, a fire broke out in the facility. Twenty-three children were displaced. Jeffrey and 11 other children were referred and admitted to Children's Shelter of Cebu, Inc (CSC), a licensed and accredited childcare agency of the Department of Social Welfare and Development.

A social worker at CSC made every effort to locate the parents, relatives or guardian of Jeffrey through public service announcements in the newspapers and on radio stations in Cebu City. These efforts failed. No one claimed Jeffrey. The authorities concluded that Jeffrey had been intentionally abandoned by his natural parents.

Jeffrey became a ward of the state on February 17, 1993 in the city of Cebu, Philippines. The Department of Social Welfare and Development became his legal guardian, "entitled to his legal custody and control, responsible for his support as defined by law, and when proper, granted the authority to give consent to his placement, guardianship, and or adoption."

The Social Case Study Report noted that Jeffrey's records, establishing him as a foundling child who was eligible for adoption, had been burned in the fire. His immunization record was lost as well. The CSC had to begin the process all over, piecing together information recorded only in the memory of caseworkers.

Jeffrey, estimated to be three years and five months, weighed just 26 pounds and stood two feet nine inches, He had a fair complexion and deeply cut dimples on both cheeks.

The childcare director reported that Jeffrey had problems controlling his emotions. "He screams in frustration if he is told that he cannot do something that he really wants to do. When he is tired, he will rock and sometimes rhythmically hit his head with his hand or arm.

"Now Jeffrey is learning the rules of the house and is cooperating with many of them. He is strong-willed and it is hard for him to give in to anything that he disagrees with. He still has temper tantrums/screaming several times each day.

"Jeffrey is learning English quite fast, responding appropriately to communication. He is a bright and inquisitive child."

A childcare worker recalled that at the time of Jeffrey's admission to The Department of Social Welfare and Development/Reception and Study Center for Children, he was "malnourished, with a fever and hard cough. Insect bites were noted all over the facial region and rashes at the perianal area." The same worker recalled that he suffered from recurring asthma. His attacks occasionally made hospitalization necessary. He was also hospitalized for diarrhea, a condition that lasted for three days.

The CSC staff suspected food allergies as Jeffrey reacted negatively to a variety of foods. He continued to cough in spite of the medications and was hospitalized for severe asthma attacks and chronic pneumonia.

The report concluded that Jeffrey Lopez was in need of "a permanent placement into a stable, loving, adoptive Christian home where his physical, psychological, and spiritual needs can be met."

Jeffrey went through a period of adjustment to his new surroundings. His care provider described him as "a strong-willed child with a mind of his own." "In the first few weeks of his stay with us, Jeffrey had a hard time. We have a set of rules for the children to obey in and out of the house. Most of what Jeffrey wanted to do was in opposition to the rules, so in the course of a day, he had several temper tantrums with a lot of screaming and pouting." The care provider also described him as "a loving and affectionate child."

Jeffrey earned the admiration of the staff during his yearlong stay because he did not let his asthma get in his way. He played hard, only slowing down to catch his breath.

My first mental picture of Jeff was one of him pulling a toy car on a string. The car, which had no wheels, was pulling a boat behind it. Jeff could make do with what he had. Nothing stopped his active imagination and his desire for fun.

1993

I first saw Jeffrey on July 28, 1993. I was nervous. Would he take one look and run away or would he hug us and say, "Hello Mommy and Daddy?"

We walked in slowly. Jeffrey ran up to us and hugged Rodney, saying, "eecallow," a baby's version of a Cebuano word meaning "I go with you." This was much better than hello. In the Philippines there is a strong bond between fathers and their children. Jeffrey gave me a quick hug and immediately went back to Rodney, who picked him up. Jeffrey promptly fell asleep in Rodney's arms. He had been as nervous about meeting us as we were about meeting him. Several sleepless nights had caught up with him. He slept for an hour while we talked to the workers.

We spent the rest of the day with Jeffrey at CSC and then prepared to go to dinner with Jeff, his friend Elmar and some shelter directors. Jeff did not understand that he was going out to dinner with us, however. The kitchen staff had made his favorite dinner, a grilled cheese sandwich. (He had the ability to get anyone to cater to him.) Now, he was torn between coming with us and eating his cheese sandwich. So he stuffed the whole sandwich into his mouth and followed us out the door. He had a way of having his sandwich and eating it too. We were all in stitches. Elmar was upset that he hadn't thought of doing the same thing.

At dinner I soon wished that I too had stuffed a cheese sandwich in my mouth. Dinner consisted of two small mussel shells per person and some veggies. To eat before dinner would be the first of many lessons Jeffrey would teach me. Jeffrey spent that night at CSC and we returned to our hotel.

I brought bags of toys and activities for Jeff to do on the fifteen-hour airplane ride home. But the plane took off and Jeff immediately fell asleep. He didn't wake up until we landed in Manila. There were four legs to the journey and Jeff slept through three of them. The last leg from Portland to Pasco was a small 17-seat plane. Jeff spent the entire time with his nose pressed against the window. He was in awe and kept talking to us. Unfortunately we had no idea what he was saying. I alone enjoyed the toys and crayons.

Friends welcomed us at the airport with balloons. Jeff was fascinated with the balloons. They fit right in with his love of all things that go up.

We told Jeff right away to ask for hugs whenever he needed them. So when he needed an extra one he would go to Rodney and say, "Up please." Rodney always obliged.

Jeff had trouble adjusting to a real bed when we first brought him home. He would often get out and sleep on the floor. One night I went to go check on Jeff and I couldn't find him. We searched the entire house. He was nowhere to be found. I finally looked one last time under his bed. All I saw was Fred, the stuffed bear, who was as big as Jeff. I pulled Fred out and there was Jeff, tucked into the corner, behind the bear, sound asleep. This behavior had to do with how he slept in the Philippines. His crib mattress there was very thin and hard. His new mattress was too soft.

Eventually we gave up trying to keep him in bed and got him a futon. That worked.

Jeff could sleep anywhere but on that soft mattress. One day Jeff was riding his plastic big wheel out in the driveway. I went inside to check on something and came back. Jeff had fallen asleep spread eagle on the cement. I could have drawn a chalk line around him.

Getting Jeff settled in the Tri-cities meant finding a doctor to treat his asthma. I found one who claimed to be a pediatric asthma specialist. On our first visit he informed me that Jeff did not have asthma—and that the doctors in the Philippines had no idea what they were talking about. I was confused. He then began questioning our choice to adopt Jeff. It was a bizarre experience and my first encounter with prejudice. Whether he was against adoptive mothers in general, opposed to multicultural adoptions, or possibly prejudiced, I never figured out.

Four weeks later the day care called and said Jeff was running a temperature. I took him to the doctor and the doctor again questioned my right to be a mother. He said that Jeff just had a cold. At 8:00 that night Jeff's temperature was so high that he had a seizure. We raced him to the emergency room. It turned out that he had pneumonia. When the ER doctor called Jeff's doctor we were informed that we had gone to the wrong hospital and he would not come to see Jeff. I asked the ER doctor if Jeff's doctor had privileges at that hospital and was informed that he did indeed. Again, was this prejudicial treatment, his judgment toward me, or rejection of Jeff? I would never know. I never saw that doctor again.

We spent a week in the hospital recuperating. I never left his side. The bed was full sized, as the hospital had no special accommodation for children. I slept right with him.

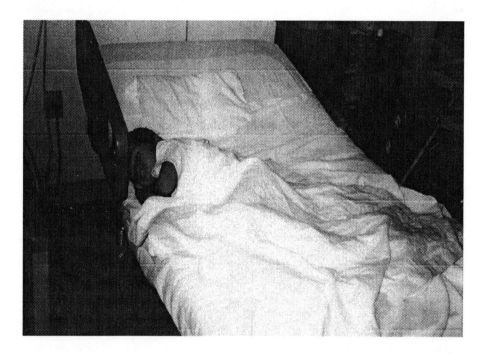

In Tacoma my sister lived across the street from a pediatric lung specialist. My mother made an appointment for us. We drove the four hours to spend five hours in his office. He said that Jeff definitely did have asthma and he wanted us to do a blood draw.

I wasn't looking forward to it. The first time Jeff had a blood draw it took three nurses to hold him down. The doctor reassured us that it would be fine. When we went into the lab we met the technician, a 6'5 Samoan. With eyes as big as saucers Jeff looked up at him and said, "You a monster." I flushed with embarrassment. The technician shrugged and said he'd been called worse by the 15-year-old who just left his office. He showed me how to hold Jeff so he could do the draw and it was over in 30 seconds, no tears shed by anyone.

In the beginning doctors were the enemy to Jeff. He would see the white coat coming and say, "Me no like you!" The first time he met his orthopedic surgeon he beaned him in the eye with his Batman figurine.

Jeff's first Christmas with us was traveling from Washington State to Rodney's family home in Dallas, North Carolina. We arrived on Christmas day. The trip was well worth it though as Mama, his grandma; fell immediately in love with Jeff. She let him watch so much T.V. that we were sure it would ruin his eyes. She fed him like Grandma only can. Jeff ate so many green beans that he pooped green. Three months into motherhood, this came as a shock. I was afraid I had ruined him.

Jeff met new cousins on this trip, and even though there was a bit of a language problem they had fun. One of his cousins, Joseph, had gotten a motorized 4-wheeler and drove Jeff all over their property. At one point Joseph let Jeff drive and Jeff took off down a hill straight for a creek. Susan, Joseph's mom, and I went running after him to catch him before he crashed. But there was no problem; Jeff turned the 4-wheeler around heading back up the hill laughing all the way.

1994

On Jeff's first Valentine's Day with us he was thrilled because he got "mail" from all his preschool friends. The candy was a bonus. Jeff would go crazy eating candy at first, but if he had any left-over, he would forget about it. He lived each moment to his fullest and didn't look back.

I loved watching Jeff learn English.

One time he was going down the stairs and fell. "Mommy, my tail hurts," he cried. I turned him around to check out his bottom. He said, "No mommy, tail," and pointed to his penis.

Another time he kept saying he needed "Bambi." I told him that we didn't have "Bambi," but we had "Beauty and the Beast." He patiently took my hand and led me to the medicine cabinet and pointed out the band-aids.

His favorite color was yellow and the y sound was difficult to master. I loved the way he said "lellow" instead of yellow.

Exactly one year from the first time we saw Jeff, Rodney and I legally became his parents. The final adoption process took about a half hour. Jeff was so nervous as we waited that he bit my leg. The judge signed the papers and said, "Congratulations." Rodney and I both said, "Thank you." Jeffrey turned to the judge and said, "Thank you, Buckwheat!" Buckwheat was my pet name for Rodney so I have to assume that Jeff liked the judge.

We went out to dinner. We were looking over the menu and I asked Jeff if he wanted chicken or spaghetti. "I already had chicken. I'll just have coffee," Jeff said. The people in the booth next to us collapsed in laughter.

1995

We moved across the state from the Tri-cities to Tacoma at the end of September. Once again Jeff got pneumonia. Fortunately, this time the doctor knew right away and we avoided a trip to the hospital. He was immediately put on antibiotics and recovered quickly.

The following September Jeff started kindergarten and L&L Learning Center for after school care. We were informed that he was very social and made lots of friends. He met his two best friends Jesse and Joe in kindergarten. Jeff loved going to school but didn't like homework. Even with extra tutoring at L&L, Jeff struggled to keep up with the other students in fine motor tasks like tying his shoes, and in intellectual tasks like counting and letter recognition. His language skills were delayed. Since he had only been speaking English for two and a half years we couldn't tell if the problem was Jeff's English or something else. His teacher was pretty impressed with his command of English though he would get confused when people spoke too quickly. If the words in a phrase were blurred together he would think they were a new word and ask for the meaning. For instance someone said "howareyou" and I had to break it down into its parts before he understood.

1996

On January 22, 1996 I picked up Jeff from L&L. When we got home, we walked in to find Rodney's suitcase still inside the front door. He had returned from a business trip the night before. I remember thinking, "Why can't he ever pick up his stuff." At that point Jeff went into the kitchen to get a snack and came immediately back out saying, "Daddy is lying on the kitchen floor." I called 911. The operator asked if a neighbor could help. I asked Jeff to run next door. We lived on a busy street and fear suddenly gripped me. I called him back, fearful of letting him out of my sight. Jeff looked at me. "It's O.K. Mom, I can do this," he calmly said.

The medics arrived within a few minutes. My sister arrived within thirty minutes. Jeff had not returned with the neighbor. I went up and down the street screaming, trying to figure out where he had gone. The neighbor came outside and said that Jeff was with his son and they were playing. The message that Jeff carried to the neighbor was, "My Daddy's lying on the kitchen floor and my mommy's crying. Could I play with Torrey?." I guess the neighbor didn't realize he was expected to do something. They were used to seeing the 911 team at our house because of Rodney's diabetes. Rodney died that day of a massive coronary.

Rodney's service was on a Friday. I wasn't sure that Jeff at age six would understand, so I let him go to school as normal. Later I wished I had taken him.

Jeff began having nightmares. He would scream and thrash and fight in his sleep. The doctor suggested that Jeff receive counseling to deal with the loss of his Dad. We set up a series of eight sessions. Through the early sessions the counselor believed that Jeff was adjusting normally. On the eighth session Jeff bit me on the hip and slapped me on the back. The counselor said, "Well, that's not normal." Jeff knew what to say and how to say it to get others to believe what he wanted them to believe. I was convinced he would become a politician. Jeff knew it was his last session and acted out. We found a new counselor.

Since the counseling did not stop the nightmares, Jeff's doctor put him on a mild sedative. It worked, however, each day when I picked Jeff up from day care he took his anger out on me. It was as though he was paying me back for being away from him. I felt that Jeff needed to focus on some-one other than me. So I decided to get a roommate. We actually got two roommates, Debbie and her daughter, Donna. Jeff liked having other peo-ple around. Donna was like a big sister to Jeff. It took a lot of pressure off our relationship. Jeff stopped yelling at me nightly. Debbie made great meatloaf and peas, Jeff's favorites.

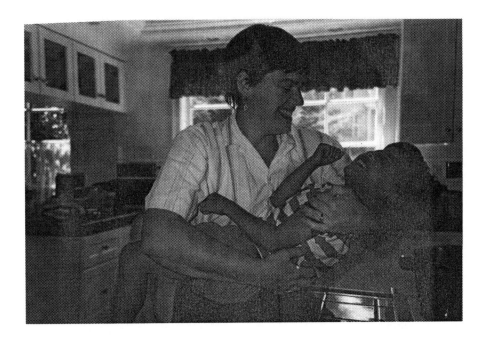

We also started our star gazing tradition. Jeff picked out a particular star and said it was Dad. He also asked if we could get a new dad, one that wasn't so old. (Rodney was only 38 when he died.) Jeff had a plan. His best friend, Jesse, was being raised by his father, who was a professional chef. This seemed like a perfect plan in Jeff's mind. I told Jeff, "That is a nice thought but James has a steady girl friend and I think he really likes her." (They later married and she became one of my best friends.)

On August 6, 1996 Jeff underwent a series of operations. He had two procedures on each ankle to create arches. They lengthened Jeff's Achilles tendon, cut some bone from the outside of his ankles and packed it on the inside of the ankles. To add insult to injury, Jeff was also circumcised the same day. I can still see him propped in the kitchen sink for a bath with his legs up in the air. My mom walked in and he said, "Look what they did to me, Grandma," pointing to his private area and disregarding his feet.

Jeff was not allowed to walk for four weeks. We borrowed a stroller from my sister. The first day of first grade fell within that time period, but he wasn't about to miss it. Jeff crawled around on his knees and the kids took turns pushing him in his stroller. The school was a brick building built at the turn of the century. One flight of stairs led up to the entrance while another led down to the cafeteria. Jeff got to eat in the classroom that day. Some friends joined him. After school we went to the orthopedic surgeon and got walking casts. The casts came off for good in October. Everything looked good and Jeff was walking okay. He still had balance issues so he could not ride a bike.

On October 25, 1996, at 8:30 P.M. a fire broke out in the reception area of our family business, Ted Brown Music Company. I was the only one available, I had to cart Jeff down with me. The fire set off the sprinklers on the main floor putting out the fire so most of the damage resulted from water and smoke. I worried about Jeff experiencing another traumatic fire event. I was also concerned with Jeff's asthma. I had to keep him as far away as possible and still be in charge. My parents were at a black-tie event up the street. They saw the smoke and rushed over followed by a few friends. Their beaded dresses and tuxedos were an interesting contrast to the hoses and fire trucks. Jeff was fascinated with the firefighters and trucks and energized by the excitement.

You would think that with all the changes that had happened in Jeff's life, it would be the big events that troubled him most. But with Jeff, it was the everyday events that created the most challenge, like adjusting to a new babysitter.

I remember the first time Rodney and I planned an evening out and hired our first sitter, a young college student. Jeffrey screamed and hollered and kicked in protest. "Don't leave me, Mommy," he cried. The sitter arrived. Jeff took one look at this beautiful dark, Italian beauty and said, in his most sincere four-year-old voice "She's beautiful. I'm gonna marry her." Later efforts to hire blonde sitters were met with great resistance. It was usually more trouble than it was worth and I took Jeff with me.

1997

It was a blessing having Debbie and Donna living with us because when I had to go out of town for business, they watched Jeff and his routine did not get interrupted.

When I returned home he would pay me back for my absence by yelling at me and refusing to do simple chores. Jeff's behavior prompted our first visit to a psychiatrist. The psychiatrist diagnosed Jeff with A.D.H.D. and recommended putting him on Ritalin. During the last two months of first grade Jeff was a different child due to the medication. He caught up on his schoolwork. He didn't act out as much when I picked him up after school. His first grade teacher, who to that point was adamantly against medication, said that this was the first time she had observed medication do what it was supposed to do.

The school did not recommend summer school, but I chose to hire a summer tutor so Jeff would not forget all he had learned during the year. The doctor took him off of Ritalin for the summer.

In September of 1997 Jeff started second grade. I needed to pick him up one day after school for a doctor's appointment. We discussed where we would meet. Jeff in all seriousness said, "You'll recognize me because I'm wearing a white shirt, black pants, and black shoes." That was the school uniform.

By October, second grade was not looking like a good year. Jeff was back on Ritalin but the effects were not as positive as they had been in first grade. I was getting calls from the school almost daily about Jeff's behavior. On October 2 the principal called asking me to pick up Jeff. Jeff was uncontrollable. He had been removed from the class for disruptive behavior, kicked the principal, ripped all the posters off the door, and was still spitting nails when I arrived. As soon as he saw me, he began to say I'm sorry, but could not explain what upset him so much. He really didn't want to go home early. When we got home all he wanted to do was sit in my lap and hug me. Sweet as sugar, yet hot as hell—that was Jeff.

The next day I took Jeff to school and sat down with his teacher and the principal to develop a plan for handling Jeff's violent moods. The nurse's station was across from the office. It had a little glass-enclosed area. They put a chair in it and called it Jeff's room. It was his time-out room.

Jeff was having these outbursts almost every day at that point and the teacher thought that the Ritalin might have caused it. So we discontinued the medicine. Jeff seemed to calm down enough to get through the rest of the year. He still had anger issues at home but could hold it together at school. Interestingly, at the end of the school year the principal retired. (She assured me that it wasn't Jeff's fault.) Also, Jeff's teacher transferred to a special education job. (She assured me that it was because of Jeff.) She was inspired by his case and wanted to help other kids with behavior issues.

Jeff was getting harder and harder to deal with at home. He wouldn't let me help him with his homework, yet he got terribly upset because he didn't know what to do. On top of that he seemed to be getting flu-like symptoms often; a runny nose, fever, and coughing. He also got pneumonia at least once each year.

1998

After Rodney passed away, I started having recurring nightmares. I dreamed that immigration officials arrived at my home to tell me that since Rodney was gone, Jeffrey no longer had two parents and that he would be removed and sent back to the Philippines. Coincidentally, I did get a letter in the mail saying that Jeff's citizenship was not finalized. I ran over to my lawyer neighbor crying that they were going to take Jeff away from me. She assured me that it was just a formality and that they were not going to take Jeff. In March of 1998 Jeff and I went up to the immigration office in Seattle. A forty-five minute process ended two years of nightmares and worry. I signed the papers and Jeff became a legal U.S. citizen.

Jeff started karate that same year. I thought it might channel some of his anger and energy. Ethan, another classmate of Jeff's, who was two belts ahead, helped Jeff. Their friendship grew. Surprisingly, Jeff liked the katas (routines) but he didn't like the fighting. They taught him how to fall without getting hurt. That was a useful skill for Jeff. Many times Jeff said, "I fell down today Mom, but I fell like they taught me in karate and I didn't get hurt." The karate helped him get stronger and become a bit more flexible. I noticed, however, that Jeff walked differently than other kids.

Jeff eventually made it to green belt, which is the sixth level. The test to get the green belt took over two hours and Jeff held it together, kept his focus, and passed with a good score.

Jeff's third grade teacher thought Jeff would do better in school if he went back on Ritalin. She thought it might calm him down. I didn't think it would help and I chose not to put him back on the medication. He was not giving the teacher any trouble, but he was also not up to grade level. He just hated to be told what to do and how to do it. His third grade teacher wore hearing aids and Jeff empathized with her. He had a heart for anyone with a disability.

Jeff and I went to Seattle for a weekend and he stopped to ask every panhandler his story. "What happened? Why can't you get a job?" Jeff asked. Most of them told him their stories; only one guy was rude. Jeff's explanation was that he needed more money. I had given Jeff $20 to spread around. He wanted more, but that was all I had at the time.

Jeff got a Nintendo for Christmas—he loved it. He could concentrate for hours on playing video games, but he couldn't apply that same attention to his class work.

1999

Because Jeff was chronically cranky the fact that it might signal that he was getting sick didn't always enter my mind. The night before I was to go on a business trip he stayed overnight with his friend Jesse. Jeff was moody, but I took that as normal for the situation. That night, Jesse's step-mom, Tamey, called to say that Jeff had a fever and needed to be picked up. I left Jeff the next day with my roommate, Debbie. She called in the afternoon saying that Jeff had chickenpox. He looked miserable but kept smiling. The crankiness had passed for the time being.

At the end of Jeff's third grade year Debbie and Donna moved out. It was back to just Jeff and me. Jeff went to horse-camp at Camp Sealth on Vashon Island; that was a mistake. He was excited to go, but overjoyed to return home. "The horses were too big." Jeff said he couldn't get up on them by himself and he feared that he would fall off. He also didn't like cleaning stalls.

When Jeff was in fourth grade I started dating Bob. Although Jeff really liked Bob, he also wanted me to himself. Schoolwork was going poorly. He kept falling further and further behind. In October Jeff said that he wished he lived with another family. I told him that was not allowed and I would not give him up. He had a dream that night that he did have a different family but was still living in our house. He didn't like that feeling. Jeff was a perfect angel, for a day and a half. Then he started getting extra mouthy. I told him I was going to wash his mouth out with soap. That evening, after he took his shower, he announced, "Soap doesn't taste very good Mom?"

"What did you do," I asked.

"I washed out my mouth with soap."

At least it wasn't as bad as the time he tried to shave with my razor.

2000

With Jeff's schoolwork continuing to decline, I took Jeff to Sylvan Learning Center to get him tested and started on a program, however, Jeff would not cooperate. They told us to come back later. The manager suggested that I put my money toward anger management for Jeff instead. We had already been seeing a counselor to help Jeff control his temper. Our efforts hadn't been successful. This counselor felt Jeff was expressing frustration at his inability to make himself understood and to understand other people. Basically, the counselor just didn't get it.

For Mother's Day that year, Jeff made me breakfast in bed-lucky charms. He was thoughtful when it came to gifts. One year he gave me a hair band because he thought the color would be pretty with my dark hair. Another year he gave me a manicure set so I wouldn't have to hunt in the drawer for my scissors.

That summer Jeff went to Star Camp through The Tacoma Actor's Guild. Of course he resisted going but unlike horse-camp, he really enjoyed it. He was more interested in the behind the scenes action than what was happening on stage. He really wanted to be the director. He liked telling people what to do and how to do it. He also enjoyed working on the set. Jeff had great artistic ability.

That summer Bob brought his three children over to the house to visit; Jeff enjoyed being part of a big family. We also got a new roommate, Anessa, who was my ballroom dance instructor. Anessa treated Jeff like her little brother. Having another person in the house once again seemed to diffuse some of Jeff's frustration.

I began noticing that Jeff fell down frequently when he started to walk fast or run. So when we went for his check-up in September, the doctor sent us back to the orthopedic surgeon. The prognosis was that Jeff had congenital hip displasia and would need surgery on both hips. We decided to do Jeff's right hip over Christmas vacation and the left one at the end of the school year.

At the end of September Bob asked me to marry him. When we told Jeff he screamed, "Noooooooo!" and started to cry. Jeff and I had a long talk. He told me that he was afraid Bob was going to die after we got married. We talked about Rodney's disease, why Rodney died, and the fact that Bob was not diabetic. I explained that although we never know how long we have, we should live life to the fullest. Jeff really did love Bob. "Bob makes you happy," Jeff told me.

On December 15 Jeff went in for the operation on his right hip. The femur was straight and it needed to be reshaped at an angle. They needed to cut the hipbone and spread it to form a cup for the femur to fit into. It was a painful operation and Jeff came out with a cast from the waist down the right leg to the ankle and down the left leg just above the knee. He was in a wheelchair for six weeks.

2001

His class was on the second floor of the school. There were no elevators. Due to insurance issues no one at the school was allowed to help. I helped Jeff walk up the stairs and then returned for the chair. The kids again took turns eating with him in his classroom since he could not negotiate the stairs without me. During a fire drill they left Jeff in the room with the understanding that in a real emergency the kids would help him down.

The cast came off in January. All looked good. You could see the lump, caused by the metal insert, through Jeff's skin because he was so skinny. That piece would come out in spring when they did the left hip.

In March we tried Sylvan again. This time Jeff cooperated. The teacher at Sylvan said they had never had anyone quite like Jeff. The regular teaching techniques were not working and they were learning to be inventive.

The week before the end of fifth grade, he went into the hospital for his left hip operation. Jeff was feeling pretty good on the last day of school so I took him in his wheelchair for the end of year celebration. The class went to a movie in a theater near school and then back to school for an ice cream party. The party was held on the playground so the kids could all be around Jeff.

Surgery left Jeff with constipation. Once when he was in the bathroom trying to go, he yelled, "It feels like I'm adopting a baby." Bob opened the door to correct him. "I know. It's a girl thing," Jeff said. Bob just closed the door and rolled his eyes.

That summer Jeff and I spent another weekend in Seattle. We walked all over downtown and Jeff did not complain once about being tired or hurting. We did have trouble crossing one intersection. Jeff's shoe slipped off and he grabbed on to my arm and we both fell into a heap on the crosswalk. We were laughing and trying to get up and get across when the light changed and the cars wanted to get through. They were honking and we were struggling to get out of their way. After we made it to the sidewalk Jeff suggested we shouldn't do that again.

For sixth grade Jeff was enrolled at Mason Middle School. He had three special education classes and three regular classes. The first semester he had social studies and band. The social studies teacher remarked that Jeff was more into the social rather than the studies. He was flunking band, which was a little frustrating for his mother who owns a music store. He was failing because he was afraid to play the solo quizzes in front of the class. He was also afraid to ask the teacher to play them after school in private. The teacher ended up giving him a pass rather than a fail because of his special education status. He did show up every day. In November, Jeff got mouthy with his school physical therapist because he said the therapist said (three times) that he walked like a monkey. Jeff then told his special education teacher that he wished he'd never been born. The school official went nuts thinking he was suicidal. So I got to take Jeff to Comprehensive Mental Health for an evaluation. That counselor thought I needed counseling and Jeff needed medication.

2002

At home things weren't going smoothly. Bob and I couldn't get on the same page about how to parent Jeff. I felt that Bob favored his own children and made different rules for Jeff. Bob did not agree. I told him, "Leave Jeff alone and let me be the parent." I felt that Bob picked fights with Jeff. Jeff also did his share of instigating fights. Once Jeff tried to hit Bob with his crutch, resulting in Bob defending himself and the crutch bent. After that I stopped leaving them alone together. I gave Bob an ultimatum. "Leave the parenting to me or leave altogether." Bob stayed. He tried to comply and would go weeks without an altercation. Then Bob would need another reminder. It was taking a toll on our marriage. I was committed to making my marriage work. I devised a plan where I would have a meal with Jeff one night and Bob the next. When I had to go out of town I left Jeff with Anessa. Jeff did not want me to have to choose one over the other and did not encourage me to end the marriage. He saw that I needed Bob and wanted me to be happy. I tried not to have Jeff feel torn apart. We looked for ways to compromise and make things work.

Jeff continued seeing his doctor regularly. At one check up the doctor diagnosed Jeff with depression and prescribed Zoloft. The doctor wanted to control Jeff's depression before prescribing medication for ADHD.

By the end of November Jeff seemed to be doing quite well on the Zoloft. Jeff and I were seeing another psychologist as well as a psychiatrist to manage Jeff's medication. In January, the psychiatrist started Jeff on Adderall for ADHD and a sleep medication, Trazodone.

Jeff's medical problems increased. Jeff's doctor noticed Jeff's toes were curling under and sent us to a neurologist. His bottom also seemed to be wasting a way and had a visible indentation. We affectionately called it his "gluteus minimus." The neurologist's diagnosis was that Jeff had neuropathy, more below his knees than elsewhere, and he had hyper-extended ligaments or loose joints. There was not much to do except design orthotics to keep Jeff's knees from back bending and keep his toes straight. As a result of the orthotics, Jeff was able to balance on a bike. Anessa taught him to ride and by June he was doing quite well. Jeff and Bob were still having problems getting along, but now Jeff had an escape. He could ride to a friend's house or over to his cousins.

In seventh grade Jeff shaped up a little. He tried to behave around Bob. He asked questions and tried to be interested in what Bob had to say. Bob was so surprised by this new behavior that he didn't know how to respond. Jeff was discouraged that his attempt to mend fences wasn't working well. He ended his pleasant spree by acting out at school and getting suspended for three days. As I remember it had something to do with a confrontation with the principal. The principal asked Jeff how he should run the school, and Jeff told him. His special ed. teacher told the principal, "If you don't want to hear the truth, don't ask Jeff."

In December of that year, my dad was diagnosed with Melanoma. This added tension to our busy and stress-filled lives. Dad became forgetful and my sister, Whitney, and I had to take over the music business much sooner than planned.

2003

By May it was obvious that the surgery on Jeff's right hip had failed. The doctor operated again. This time the surgeon cut the pelvis and rotated it to give more of a socket and cut more of the femur. Jeff's right leg was then three quarters of an inch shorter than his left. The doctor diagnosed the beginnings of scoliosis as well. Jeff had to have a tutor for the last month of classes. He greatly preferred only one and a half hours of class versus a full day. Jeff's friend Trevor would come over most days and keep Jeff entertained by playing Nintendo. Jeff got very good at all his games.

Jeff was out of the cast for our summer vacation. We met my three sisters and their families on Edisto Island, South Carolina. Not only did Jeff get to visit with all his cousins and aunts and uncles, he also got to visit his "Mama," Rodney's mother, who still lived in North Carolina. Jeff had a great time on the beach, finding lots of shark teeth. This seems to be the big thing, well maybe the only thing, to do on Edisto Island besides playing in the ocean. Jeff had to take his crutches with him wherever he went and that included the beach. When we were in the ocean one of us would always be holding onto Jeff so he wouldn't get washed away. Jeff still had a great time.

The transition into Eighth grade was smooth. Jeff, however soon started getting anxious about going on to high school. He stopped attempting his schoolwork hoping to be held back. We told him he was going to be sent on to high school whether he passed or not because he was designated as special education. As a result Jeff shaped up and graduated from eighth grade without further complication.

2004

My mom and dad came to Jeff's eighth grade graduation ceremony. Bob showed up late and stood at the back. Jeff was last in the procession. His class gave him a standing ovation when he went up to get his certificate of completion.

After the ceremony girls kept coming up to Jeff asking if he remembered them. Jeff was so proud. His grin stretched from ear to ear like the Joker in Batman. Jeff had recently begun to notice girls and asked repeatedly how to get a girlfriend. I kept telling him to be himself and amazing things would happen. That night proved my point as the girls thronged around him.

That summer Jeff started glass blowing class at Wilson High School as part of the Hilltop Artists program. It was supposed to be a three-week class, but Jeff was enjoying himself so much that the teacher suggested he stay for another three weeks. When school started in the fall, Jeff continued to take the glass blowing class after school.

In October of ninth grade, while Bob and I were in Hawaii trying to work things out, Jeff had an altercation at school. He called his social studies teacher a bitch. My mother had to go pick him up from school and take him to Anessa's apartment where he was staying. Jeff wouldn't tell anyone at school why he had done what he did, but he told Anessa that he was defending a friend when some other kids were putting their feet on his friend's desk and chair. Jeff was the only one caught and punished. He was suspended for a day.

Jeff and I talked about the possibility of enrolling in the Tacoma School of the Arts, a special magnet school, for tenth grade. The school has a close connection to the Museum of Glass and the hot shop at the museum. I liked the idea that it was a small school with mentoring classes every Friday. We took a tour and spoke to some students. Jeff was thrilled. The application was long and the interviews longer. But Jeff did not get upset at any of the timed drawing quizzes or the length of the two interviews.

In December, my father took a drastic turn for the worst. Bob brought Jeff to the hospital and Jeff was able to say good-bye to "Papa." Jeff gave him a piece of glass that he had blown. My dad was in a coma and could not see the glass paperweight, but Jeff rubbed the cool glass against his cheek and told him that he loved him. This meant a lot to Jeff, as he had not had a chance to tell his own dad good-bye. My dad died that day, December 11, 2004.

2005

In January, Jeff got accepted to the School of the Arts. The only stipulation was that he had to pass ninth grade. Jeff said he was going to work harder and not cause any more problems. His grades improved.

In March, my friend Rebekka's daughter, Teddi went through her Bat mitzvah, the Jewish rite of passage for girls. I went to New York to attend and help. Jeff stayed home with my mom and Anessa. Jeff and Mom got along great while I was gone. Jeff spent Monday night with Anessa. Tuesday the school called, saying that Jeff did not feel well and someone needed to take him home. I got home from New York later on Tuesday afternoon. Jeff was sleeping. Wednesday morning I let him sleep instead of going to school because he said his neck hurt. I thought he might have gotten a knot in his neck from sleeping on Anessa's couch. Jeff wanted to go to the doctor on Wednesday evening. The doctor listened closely for pneumonia since it was typical with Jeff. He didn't hear anything and said his throat was a bit red and tested him for strep throat. The test was negative. The doctor said if he didn't feel better in a few days it could be mononucleosis. The only way to check immediately was to take a blood test. Jeff did not want that done.

When we got home from the doctor's office, Jeff seemed to perk up. He had a great dinner, played video games, and acted more lively. Thursday morning he got up and had breakfast. He said his neck still kind of hurt. He whined all the way to school. We bypassed school and I took him to work with me. He slept on the couch in the lunchroom. We went home about 2:00 in the afternoon. He perked up again, ate a great dinner, and played video games.

03/19/2005

Friday the same thing happened. I took him to work with me. He felt crumby in the morning but was fine by afternoon.

On Saturday Jeff woke up feeling okay. He wanted his friend, Trevor, to stay overnight. I told him, "Let's wait until you're better."

On Sunday Jeff seemed worse. I called the doctor at his home. He said if Jeff wasn't better by Monday morning to bring Jeff in for a check-up.

I went to Easter service and came home to get Jeff ready to go to my sister's house for Easter dinner. I helped him get on his pants. He started whining and complaining about going. I left him home and went to my sister's.

I started having this awful feeling that I needed to go home. The family talked me into staying to eat. When they encouraged me to stay for cake I said, "I'm going home." When I got home Jeff was sleeping fitfully and it sounded like he was having difficulty breathing. Jeff slept deeply and was often hard to wake up. Yet, this seemed different than usual. The concern nagged at me.

I called the doctor again and left a message. The doctor called back saying he didn't think it was anything to worry about, but maybe I should take him to Mary Bridge Children's Hospital to ease my mind.

Bob managed to get Jeff into the car, despite Jeff's kicking and screaming objections. As I said earlier, Jeff's strong will never left him. I drove Jeff to Mary Bridge. When we arrived I asked one of the attendants to help get Jeff out of the car. The attendant got Jeff into the wheelchair, and parked it next to the triage nurse.

The ER was packed. The triage nurse, who was helping someone else, kept looking over at Jeff. Finally she asked the father of the little girl she was helping if they could step aside so she could help Jeff. She hooked up a devise that calculates the oxygen in the blood; bells and whistles went off. Three attendants appeared. All of a sudden we were rushed to the back. When they moved another girl out of the way, I started to get nervous.

An X-ray showed that 75 percent of his lungs were full of pneumonia. He was operating on 25 percent of the oxygen he needed to function. They looked at me as if to say, "Why did you wait so long?"

They began asking questions about his meds. By this time Jeff was putting up a fuss. "Don't stick me with needles. Get that mask away; I just want to go home," he demanded.

The doctors said that with his low oxygen level he shouldn't have been able to speak let alone remember who he was. As I listed his meds, Jeff piped up. "Don't forget the Trazodone!"

They wanted to stick a tube down Jeff's throat to help him breathe. He did not want that. He begged me not to let them do it, but neither Jeff nor I had any control at this point. By then they had already given him a shot to put him to sleep.

We took him upstairs to the PICU and put him on all the monitors. They kept telling me it was bad. I figured, "You just don't know Jeff. You don't know what he has gone through to be in this world." I could not imagine that a little pneumonia would stop him. He had battled pneumonia so many times already. But I guess his body was just too tired to fight it. The antibiotics didn't do a thing. Jeff had gotten there too late.

They told me it was going to be a long wait and that I would be there for weeks if anything worked. I went home to grab a book to read to Jeff because they told me he could still hear us. While I was home I took about an hour nap. The fact that I could grab a nap says that I had confidence that Jeff would be okay. I knew his fighting spirit.

When I got back to his room, everything was quiet. I had been told that if none of the staff was in the room except the nurse, it was a good sign. About six o'clock Monday morning my mom showed up. I went outside to talk to her as the staff went in to turn Jeff from his stomach to his back. I couldn't watch. There were tubes everywhere.

When mom and I came back in, the whole world was in the room. The tides had turned. They performed CPR on Jeff. Everyone moved at lightening speed.

A family friend, Jenny Rake-Marona, who is also an associate pastor at my church, was in the room encouraging Jeff to hang on. Jenny's son, Spencer, and Jeff were going to be attending the Tacoma School of the Arts together in the fall. It was a comfort to have her there at this critical time.

The hospital staff wanted to try to transport Jeff to Children's Hospital in Seattle where there was a heart-lung bypass machine. Mary Bridge wasn't due for a unit for another couple of months. The doctors tried to stabilize Jeff to get him up to the helicopter pad. As soon as they got him stabilized and ready to be moved, Jeff's heart stopped again. They stabilized him again.

Around 11:00 they took him to the Helicopter pad. Jeff's heart stopped again. This time they could not bring him back.

I left him and I feel so guilty. Thoughts ran through my head. "I shouldn't have left him to go down to my sister's house. How am I supposed to live without him?" It doesn't matter that everyone tells me I did all I could do.

On Wednesday of that week the doctor did not detect any pneumonia. I was told that this is what happens to people who have an immune deficiency and don't get pneumonia treated in the early stages. Jeff, however, didn't have an immune deficiency. We still have no idea why his body was unable to fight the pneumonia.

2006

Today I am left with my memories. I believe Jeff came to teach patience and to show us how to play and have fun. He demanded joy from all of us. He also valued honesty and that included his relationship with God. In the midst of suffering he asked once, "Who invented pain?" My answer at the time did not satisfy him and I have to admit I still struggle with why he had to suffer. I believed that I held his destiny in my hands, so I tried to train him and arrange for his happiness. But in reality, Jeff was the master of his own destiny and we were captives to "Jeff Time." His life was a blessing, a gift to those who knew him and an unexpected treasure for those who will read his story.

Anniversaries are difficult for me. Just before the anniversary of Jeff's death I called a psychic to confirm my belief that Jeff was happy and in a better place. She told me that Jeffrey was happy and that he was riding his bike everywhere. I smiled deep inside. You see, Jeffrey was only able to ride his bike one summer due to his increasing problems with his hips. Close to Mother's Day I stopped in at a local café. They had a tarot card reader set up in the corner. People who have experienced loss like I have readily accept comfort in any form that it takes. I sat down to have a reading. "Jeff is at peace and happy and with the angels," she said. She said that many angels are around me as well. She said he is with family. His dad and his papa, my father, preceded Jeff in death.

I don't blame anyone for Jeffrey's death including God.

Jeff had many friends in his life, but he had known Joe since kindergarten. On the day of Jeff's death, Joe was watching South Park. In the series, Kenny is always dying and going to heaven. In this episode Kenny died because God needed the best video game player. "Maybe that was true for Jeffrey," Joe said. Jeff was constantly playing video games. He was good at them. He tried to get me to play once. Handing me the controls, he said

"Now Mom all you have to do is press A-B-B-A." That sounded easy enough. But the controls rumbled in my hands and scared me. I threw them up into the air. Jeff laughed and said, "Never mind."

It was surprising how many kids were at Jeff's service and how many stood up to talk. Everyone at school seemed to know Jeff.

The students at Stadium High School thought Jeff was such an inspiration that they created an award in his honor. Each year, on Memorial Day, a freshman at Stadium High School is now presented the Jeffrey Ray Eidson Award. His or her name is engraved on a memorial plaque in Jeff's memory. The award is given to a student who displays the qualities that the students saw in Jeffrey: inspirational, outgoing, and ability to overcome adversity. The recipient also displays tremendous growth, maturity, and a sense of humor.

When the plaque was presented to me at the annual Memorial Day ceremony, I was deeply touched. It was so nice to know that they thought of Jeff in the same way as I did. They knew and accepted Jeff, quirks and all.

The funeral home set up a web page where folks could express their feelings about Jeff. Many of his fellow students, staff, and interested friends took time to share their memories.

I've known you since sixth grade. You were the funniest and most intelligent man. In seventh grade at Mason Middle School especially when me and Mickayla would come back from lunch, you were there and you would talk the whole time. It was funny because we had someone to cheer us up. I will always remember that big smile.
Tanya

You were a good friend of both of ours. We truly do miss your smile and your funny jokes and laughing at everything. You are an inspiration to us as you did your work and got good grades and never let anyone put you down. We love you so much Jeff. We're sorry to see you go so soon.
Amy and Angela

The halls at Stadium will be a lot quieter and lonely knowing that you will not be there to cheer us up.
Jessica

I will always remember him for his smile. That smile was so big that it could brighten anybody's day.
Christina

Jeff will always be a symbol of the human spirit to never give up no matter the odds.
Football Coach

Jeff had a spirit and life about him that was not dampened by his difficulties. All students are special but Jeffrey is one who has remained vital in my memory.
Jeffrey's second grade teacher

I was shocked and saddened to hear that Jeff has gone home to be with the Lord. My heart goes out to you Stephanie, I remember well the day you came here to meet Jeff for the first time and take him home with you. Jeff will always be a CSC KID in our hearts! You can count on prayers of support and help in your grief from us here in Cebu City. God bless all of you there who loved Jeffrey!!!
Sandy Swanson Child Development Director at CSC

Jeffrey's humor, intelligence, and perceptive mood are preserved in his drawings and cartoons.

Memorial Service for
Jeffrey Eidson
April 1, 2005
Immanuel Presbyterian Church
Reprinted by permission
Rev. Jenny Rake-Marona

"Let the little children come to me, and do not stop them; for it is to such as these that the kingdom of heaven belongs." Matthew 19:14

Welcome on behalf of Stephanie and Bob, all of Jeff's family and the community of faith here at Immanuel Presbyterian Church, I am privileged to welcome you to this service of worship and memory. Today we are gathered to honor the life and the spirit of Jeffrey Ray Eidson; your son, grandson, nephew, cousin, and friend. Being here at this moment is so important; it is our time to celebrate the gift of his life, to help each other with the unwelcome task of saying goodbye to him, and to give witness to the gift of the resurrection, which is God's gift of new life for Jeffrey and for all of us.

I would like to invite you now, to take a moment to quiet your minds and hearts, to relax just a bit, to take a deep breath and feel the solid ground beneath your feet. Take this moment to fully arrive, here; in this sacred time and place and know that God meets us here to help and to heal and to hold us as we remember.

Homily

"Jeffrey had energy like a lightening bolt," said Donna, his former Cub Scout leader. "It was what made him creative. That was the magic of Jeffrey."

I couldn't agree more and I am so grateful for the image. Jeff was bright and intense. His impact was quick and it packed a wallop. My experience of Jeff was like watching the summer storms roll through when we lived in Savannah, Georgia; bright, blue skies, clouds in the distance, gathering winds, rising pressure fronts, a hint of electricity in the air, a clap of thunder, a burst of light, a sunshine, clouds breaking up, a quiet breeze and clear blue skies again. You never knew exactly when the storm would happen, but you always knew it would.

With Jeffrey, all of life was like a summer storm. When I asked his mom and grandma to describe the "essence" of Jeffrey, they said, "He was sweet as pie and hot as Hell!" It's not everyone who can embody both ends of the spectrum like that, but Jeff truly did. He was passionate about justice, for himself and for others. Stephanie tells a story about walking down Pike Street in Seattle with Jeff several years ago. She said it took forever because he insisted on asking every homeless man on the street to tell him their story. Then he insisted on giving each one of them some money. (I'm not sure Stephanie came prepared for that part of the adventure!) An injustice done to someone else or to him could trigger a tidal wave of anger that was best calmed by the equal strength of one of his "other mothers", Anessa.

Jeff lived daily with challenges that most of us never even imagine bumping up against. From the time he was a little boy, he lived with chronic pain in his legs and hips that limited his activity. He also lived with the impact of Attention Deficit Disorder, which made it hard for him to focus and learn and to develop relationships with teachers and peers. Yet, he met each of these challenges with a mix of tenacity and determination, moments of frustration and his own lively sense of humor. He had a collection of T-shirts that revealed a bit of his outlook on things. One shows a tumbling stick figure, and reads, "I do all my own stunts." The other says, "They say I have A.D.D., but they just don't understand…. Oh, look! There goes a chicken!"

Most recently, Jeffrey had found within himself the capacity to take on these challenges and to work toward two very important goals: acceptance into the Tacoma School of the Arts and getting his driver's license. With these goals in front of him he went through a lengthy application and interview process and made strides in classes and relationships with teachers that were absolutely essential if he wanted to reach his goals. Well, he did get accepted to TSOTA and last Saturday he got his latest progress report. "Jeffrey is a pleasure to have in this class," each teacher said. "Jeffrey is making significant progress in his work." Ah, sweet success!

Today we are here to give thanks for the gift of Jeffrey Eidson's life, his whole life. As we talked a night or two ago, his family and I were struck by the paradoxes that made up the truth of his being; he was sweet and hot, happy and angry, light and dark. He had A.D.D. and possessed an artist's capacity to attend to detail. Every day was a mix of pain and pleasure, love and hate. And Jeff did not shrink from any of them. When he was mad, he let you know. If he figured God was to blame for all his pain, he let you know that, too. If he was happy, you could almost feel the warmth in the bright blaze of his smile. Life was not easy for Jeff, but, as Donna said, that struggle was what made him who he was. If we are honest with ourselves, I think we might all discover that there is much to be learned from Jeffrey about the willingness to take on all of life and all of ourselves, to struggle with the dark side of our being in order to nourish the light. Jeffrey was God's gift to each of us and if we pay attention, we will all be the better for having known him.

The most difficult part of being here today, is the task of acknowledging Jeff's death. None of us would ever have guessed that we would be in this place for this purpose today. It is virtually impossible to accept the end of a life that comes so suddenly and so early. It goes against all our instincts. We resist letting the truth in; we shield ourselves from fully embracing the reality. Our sadness, anger and even our fears rise up inside us and we do our best to defend ourselves against them.

What I want you to know is that that is completely natural and even healthy. It's the way our psyche, perhaps even our soul, protects us against something too huge to completely comprehend. I have often heard it said that grief is like a fog that engulfs us, and that it lifts ever so slowly, gradually allowing us to take in the truth one little bit at a time and to heal. Today you may feel like the fog is particularly thick. If you think of it as a gift, it may be less frightening and you won't have to work so hard to fight your way out of it. It will lift naturally as you do the work of mourning, of saying goodbye and letting go.

That is why it is so important that we are all here today, gathered as a community of faith, family and friends. What a powerful gathering! Together you will tell the stories, remember the good times and the hard times. You will spark in each other the essence of Jeff's spirit and you will refine and distill your memories until you have those most treasured jewels of what it meant to be Jeff's mom or grand-mom, step-dad, cousin, aunt, uncle and friend. You may learn from your struggles with him. You may laugh and cry together. Together we will listen and tell and transform our sorrow in such a way that our memories become part of our lives, so that Jeff lives on in us as we move forward with our living.

This brings us to one last thing, the Resurrection, the gift of new life that is God's gift to Jeff and to each of us as well.

Many of you may remember the day that Jeff was baptized here in this church. This was before my time, but Stephanie told me about it at the hospital the other day. It was the Sunday before Christmas, 1996. Jeff was seven years old and Stephanie remembers that Pastor Paul Galbreath made an extra effort to douse him with a lot of water, two hands full, so that Jeff would really feel the wetness on his head through that amazing head of thick hair. Well, I guess he was soaked! Stephanie says Jeff looked up with water dripping off him, and with that big grin on his face, said, "Can I get a towel, please?" On that day, Stephanie's and Jeffrey's community gathered around and celebrated his membership in the family of faith. We affirmed that Jeff belonged to God and always would. Today we reaffirm Jeff's place in the heart of God. Pure of spirit and whole of body, Jeff is one with God and with all who have died before him. In fact, there is a bit of a debate about what they are doing right now, but Jeff's family is certain that he has been met by his dad, Rodney and his grandfather, Warren: all three healed, reconciled and reunited, joined to the life of God forever.

Resurrection is God's gift to us as well—we, who must now continue with our living, through the fog, in the midst of occasional summer storms, despite or perhaps refined by our own personal pains and challenges. I can't help but remember that we are less than one week away from the dark tunnel of Holy Week and the glory of Easter morning. During Holy Week we remember that God, in Christ, shares our suffering. God knows our sadness, even grieves the death of an only son. On Easter we remember that nothing, nothing, nothing can separate us from the love of God in Christ, not even death. This afternoon and every day God's spirit meet us to breathe the breath of love and new life into our spirits into our very bodies so that we too might rise again and live. Thanks be to God.

Benediction

May the God of hope fill you with all peace in believing, so that you may abound in hope by the power of the Holy Spirit. May the love of God the creator, the grace of Christ our redeemer, and the fellowship of the Holy Spirit be with us now and always. Alleluia. Amen.

978-0-595-44324-6
0-595-44324-9

Printed in the United States
79746LV00005BA/109-156